cont

GW00707450

British & North American Readers:
Please note that Australian cup and
spoon measurements are metric. A quick
conversion guide appears on page 63.
A glossary explaining unfamiliar terms
and ingredients begins on page 60.

adding fresh flavour

Fresh herbs are always better to use than dried herbs which can have a musty taste, particularly if they're old. However, since most herbs are seasonal and you have to use dried in winter, use 1 teaspoon dried for every tablespoon chopped fresh herbs. These are not all herbs: some are spices, some are fruits, but they all add wonderful flavour to your cooking.

Basil

Most well-known for its use in pesto, basil also has a natural affinity with tomatoes. Shred and sprinkle over tomato salads just before serving, or add whole small leaves to a green salad. Basil has a peppery taste, and its flavour increases when cooked.

Coriander

Also known as cilantro, the fresh leaves and roots are regarded as a herb; the dried seeds are a spice. Don't try to substitute ground seeds for fresh leaves or vice versa — the flavours are completely different. Fresh coriander, which looks similar to flat-leaf parsley, has a pungent aroma and a peppery taste; it is commonly used in Asian and Mexican dishes.

Chives

Chives add a fresh onion flavour to potato salad, egg salad and scrambled eggs, and they're a great garnish for creamy soups, especially if a spoonful of cream or sour cream is added just before serving. Finely chop and scatter over casseroles or sprinkle over the sour cream topping on a baked potato. Chives are best if eaten raw: cut them into tiny pieces with scissors or a very sharp knife.

Oregano

Greek and Italian cooking make liberal use of fresh oregano. It has a strong flavour that goes particularly well with vegetable and meat dishes such as moussaka, tomato-based sauces, Greek salad and pizza.

Chilli

A fruit rather than a herb, chilli is used in Mexican food and as an aromatic along with garlic and ginger in many Asian recipes. As a general rule, the smaller the chilli, the greater its heat. Removing the membranes and seeds reduces the heat. Wash hands thoroughly after handling chillies or wear rubber gloves: chilli oil can irritate the skin.

Mint

Familiar for its use in cooking peas and new potatoes, in mint sauce for lamb and as a garnish for iced tea, the fresh (minty) taste of mint is also delicious in fruit juices, especially fresh pineapple juice, fruit salad and as a hot tea with honey.

Lemon grass

Only the white part at the bulb end of the stem is used in cooking (although all parts can be used to make lemon-grass tea). Lemon grass has a fresh, strong sour-lemon taste and cooking enhances its flavour. Use in Asian salads and soups.

Marjoram

Similar to oregano but not as strong in flavour, fresh marjoram is delicious in Italian beef stews cooked with tomatoes, meat loaves and rissoles. Wild marjoram, called rigani, is used in Greek cooking.

Bay leaf

Indispensable in a bouquet garni (a bay leaf and a sprig each of thyme and parsley placed in a little muslin bag and used to flavour soups and casseroles), bay leaves can be used fresh or dried. Infuse them in milk when making a white sauce or store a leaf or two in a jar of rice — it imparts a delicious flavour to rice pudding.

Sage

Sage has traditionally been used with fatty food such as pork and duck. It is reputed to aid the digestion of such rich food. It is also part of the most famous of stuffings for roast poultry: sage and onion stuffing. Use sparingly because its flavour tends to dominate.

4

Dill

Fresh dill with its feathery leaves is ideal with egg, potato and fish dishes. It is often used in Scandinavian cooking, particularly in pickles and in gravlax (preserved raw salmon). It has a delicate, slightly aniseed taste and is best eaten raw or added to food at the last minute. Try chopped dill sprinkled over cucumber and sour cream salad.

Ginger

Dried powdered ginger is a spice, but the fresh root is used as an aromatic. Do not try to substitute one for the other — their flavours are quite different. Fresh ginger is used extensively in Asian cooking, often first heated with garlic and chilli to release its flavour. Peel a piece of ginger root and slice, chop or grate it according to the recipe's requirements.

Rosemary

Rosemary is a spiky plant so chop the leaves finely when using in cooked dishes or use whole sprigs which can be removed before serving. Rosemary is most well-known for its affinity with lamb. Try it with any strong-flavoured meat or with vegetables such as zucchini and eggplant. Always use rosemary in moderation: it can be overpowering.

Parsley

The two most familiar types of parsley are curly-leaf and flat-leaf. Flat-leaf has more flavour and is more versatile — as well as the flavour it imparts in cooking, the whole leaves of flat-leaf parsley are a delicious addition to green salads, and are indispensable in tabbouleh.

flat-leaf parsley

curly-leaf parsley

Watercress
Delicious and nutty-tasting, watercress can be eaten raw in salads, cooked and pureed like spinach, or made into a creamy soup with potatoes and chicken stock.

Tarragon
Most commonly used as a flavouring for vinegar, in béarnaise sauce or with chicken dishes, tarragon is also good in a buttery sauce for artichokes. There are two types of tarragon: French and Russian. French is by far the most flavoursome and is the one most often used in cooking.

Rocket
A peppery, nutty, green salad herb. When young, the leaves are quite mild; they become more bitter as they grow and are especially so after flowering. Use in mixed salads or on its own as a salad with shaved parmesan and a lemon and oil dressing.

Garlic
A strongly flavoured herb, garlic may be eaten raw, in garlic mayonnaise (aioli) and garlic butter, or cooked. The longer it cooks, the milder its flavour. Roasted garlic has a sweet flavour and is delicious when slipped out of its skin and spread on steak, lamb or crostini (bread slices brushed with olive oil and toasted).

Thyme
There are several varieties of thyme, but the most common is garden thyme. Use it in casseroles and other hearty dishes, either by stripping the leaves off the stems, or by tying in a muslin bag with a bay leaf and a sprig or two of parsley (bouquet garni). It is also excellent with potatoes. Use sparingly.

6

chive and pepper
chicken

4 (600g) chicken thigh cutlets

¹/₄ cup (60g) seeded mustard

2 tablespoons drained green peppercorns, chopped

2 cloves garlic, crushed

2 tablespoons lemon juice

¹/₄ cup chopped fresh chives

1 tablespoon olive oil

1 small (80g) brown onion, chopped

Remove and discard skin from chicken; place chicken in large bowl, coat with combined mustard, peppercorns, garlic, juice, chives and half the oil.

Heat remaining oil in large pan; cook onion until soft. Add chicken to pan; cook, turning once and brushing chicken on both sides with peppercorn mixture, until chicken is browned all over and cooked through.

Per serve fat 10g; fibre 1.3g; kJ 802

8 navarin of lamb

1kg lean diced lamb

2 cloves garlic, crushed

2 tablespoons plain flour

1 tablespoon vegetable oil

³/₄ cup (180ml) chicken stock

¹/₃ cup (80ml) dry white wine

1 tablespoon tomato paste

8 baby (200g) onions

1 sprig fresh rosemary

2 sprigs fresh thyme

2 bay leaves

1 bunch (300g) baby carrots

3 small (270g) turnips, quartered

2 tablespoons roughly chopped flat-leaf parsley

Toss lamb in large bowl with garlic and flour. Heat oil in large pan; cook lamb in batches until just browned. Return lamb to pan; add stock, wine, paste, onion, rosemary, thyme and bay leaves. Bring to boil; simmer, covered, 1³/4 hours.
Add carrots and turnip; simmer, covered, about 45 minutes or until lamb and vegetables are tender.
Just before serving, stir in parsley.

Per serve fat 14.5g; fibre 6g; kJ 1820

10 veal and vegetable parcels with marjoram

4 x 125g veal steaks

1 small (70g) carrot

125g mushrooms, sliced

1 teaspoon soy sauce

1 tablespoon fresh marjoram leaves

2 teaspoons tomato paste

1/2 cup (125ml) chicken stock

1/4 cup (60ml) evaporated skim milk

Pound steaks thinly with meat mallet. Cut carrot into thin strips. Place carrot, mushrooms, soy sauce, marjoram, tomato paste and stock in a medium pan; bring to boil, simmer 3 minutes. Strain; reserve liquid.

Divide vegetable mixture between steaks, fold in sides, roll up into parcels; tie with string. Return reserved liquid to pan, reheat, add veal parcels, simmer about 10 minutes or until tender. Remove parcels from pan; keep warm.

Add evaporated milk to liquid in pan, heat without boiling. Remove string from veal parcels. Cut parcels into slices. Serve with sauce.

Per serve fat 2.5g; fibre 1.5g; kJ 683

stir-fried tofu with
satay sauce

Cut tofu into 2cm pieces. Combine garlic, ginger, lemon grass, sauce and juice in large bowl, add tofu, mix gently. Cover, refrigerate 2 hours. Drain; reserve marinade.

Heat oil in wok or large pan, stir-fry tofu until lightly browned; remove from wok. Add bok choy, sprouts, snow peas and coriander to wok, stir-fry about 2 minutes or until bok choy is just wilted. Stir in reserved marinade, then tofu, stir gently over heat until heated through. Serve drizzled with Satay Sauce; top with crushed peanuts.

Satay Sauce Combine all ingredients in small pan, stir over low heat until smooth and heated through.

Per serve fat 9g; fibre 4g; kJ 596

500g firm tofu

2 cloves garlic, crushed

1 teaspoon grated fresh ginger

1 tablespoon finely chopped fresh lemon grass

2 tablespoons soy sauce

$1/4$ cup (60ml) lime juice

2 teaspoons peanut oil

1 bunch (340g) baby bok choy, shredded

2 cups (160g) bean sprouts

150g snow peas, sliced

$1/4$ cup chopped fresh coriander leaves

2 tablespoons crushed peanuts

satay sauce

$1/3$ cup (85g) smooth peanut butter

$1/2$ cup (125ml) light coconut cream

1 tablespoon brown sugar

1 tablespoon mild sweet chilli sauce

2 teaspoons lime juice

$1/2$ cup vegetable stock

12 irish stew with herb
dumplings

750g lean diced lamb

2 tablespoons plain flour

1 teaspoon freshly ground black pepper

2 large (400g) brown onions, sliced

2 large (600g) potatoes, sliced

1 large (180g) carrot, sliced

1/2 cup (100g) pearl barley

2 teaspoons finely chopped fresh thyme

1 1/2 cups (375ml) vegetable stock

1 litre (4 cups) hot water

herb dumplings

1 cup (150g) self-raising flour

40g cold butter, chopped

1 tablespoon finely chopped fresh parsley

1 tablespoon finely chopped fresh thyme

1 egg, beaten

1/4 cup (60ml) skim milk, approximately

Toss lamb in large bowl with combined flour and pepper.

Layer half the onion, potato, carrot and lamb in large heavy-based pan; repeat layering with the remaining vegetables and lamb. Sprinkle with barley and thyme; pour over combined stock and water. Bring to boil; skim surface of stew. Simmer, covered, for 1 1/2 hours.

Uncover stew; drop heaped tablespoons Herb Dumpling mixture, 2cm apart, on top. Cover stew; simmer about 15 minutes or until dumplings are cooked through.

Herb Dumplings Place flour in medium bowl; rub in butter. Stir in herbs, egg and enough milk to mix to a soft, sticky dough.

Per serve fat 12g; fibre 6g; kJ 1911

14 fish salad

with lime dressing

500g white fish fillets

8 mignonette lettuce leaves

175g watercress

4 (140g) radishes, sliced thinly

2 medium (240g) carrots, chopped

1 medium (200g) red capsicum, chopped

lime dressing

1 teaspoon grated lime rind

1 teaspoon grated fresh ginger

1 tablespoon lime juice

1/3 cup (80ml) no-oil French dressing

2 teaspoons chopped fresh chives

Cut fish into bite-size pieces, place in small pan, cover with water. Bring to boil, simmer, uncovered, about 2 minutes or until fish is cooked through; drain. Place fish and Lime Dressing in a large bowl; refrigerate several hours or overnight.

Combine remaining ingredients in a serving bowl, add undrained fish, toss lightly.

Lime Dressing Place ingredients in small bowl, mix well to combine.

Per serve fat 4g; fibre 5 g; kJ 770

tuna with coriander
pesto

4 thick (800g) tuna steaks

coriander pesto

1/2 cup firmly packed fresh coriander leaves

1 tablespoon peanut oil

2 tablespoons boiling water

1 tablespoon unsalted roasted peanuts

1 small fresh red chilli, seeded, chopped

2 tablespoons lime juice

2 teaspoons wasabi paste

Brush tuna with half the Coriander Pesto. Cook tuna on heated oiled griddle pan or barbecue until browned both sides and just cooked through.

Serve tuna with reserved Coriander Pesto.

Coriander Pesto Blend or process all ingredients until just smooth.

Per serve fat 12g; fibre 1g; kJ 1206

16 chickpea and beef
salad

1/2 cup (80g) burghul

1 tablespoon olive oil

500g piece beef eye fillet

2 x 310g cans chickpeas, rinsed, drained

2 (260g) Lebanese cucumbers, chopped

2 medium (400g) red capsicums, chopped

1 tablespoon chopped fresh coriander leaves

2 tablespoons chopped fresh mint leaves

4 green onions, chopped

1 medium (150g) brown onion, sliced finely

1 small fresh red chilli, seeded, chopped finely

dressing

2 tablespoons fish sauce

1/4 cup lemon juice

1 clove garlic, crushed

1 teaspoon grated lemon rind

Place burghul in heatproof bowl, cover with hot water, stand 20 minutes. Drain, rinse under cold water; drain and spread out on absorbent paper.
Heat oil in medium pan, add beef, cook over high heat on all sides until well browned; reduce heat, cook until beef is cooked as desired; drain, cover, cool. Cut beef into thin strips.
Combine chickpeas, burghul, beef, cucumber, capsicum, coriander, mint, both onions and chilli in large bowl. Drizzle with Dressing just before serving.
Dressing Combine all ingredients in jar.

Per serve fat 12g; fibre 6g; kJ 1326

capsicum sauce

1 small (230g)
eggplant

coarse sea salt

600g veal fillet, sliced

2 teaspoons butter

2 cloves garlic,
crushed

1 medium (150g)
brown onion, chopped

1 medium (200g) red
capsicum, chopped

400g can tomatoes

1 tablespoon chopped
fresh basil leaves

2 teaspoons chopped
fresh oregano leaves

2 teaspoons olive oil

$^1/_4$ cup (20g) grated
fresh parmesan
cheese

Cut eggplant
lengthways into 1cm
slices, place over wire
rack, sprinkle with
salt; stand 30 minutes.
Rinse eggplant under
cold water, pat dry
with absorbent paper.
Place veal between
pieces of plastic wrap,
pound out thinly. Heat

butter in a large pan,
add garlic, onion and
capsicum, cook,
stirring, 5 minutes or
until capsicum is soft.
Stir in undrained
crushed tomatoes,
basil and oregano.
Bring to boil, simmer,
uncovered, about
8 minutes or until
mixture is thickened
slightly. Blend or
process tomato
mixture in batches
until smooth.
Heat a 6-cup (1.5-litre)
capacity flameproof
dish, brush lightly with
some of the oil,
cook veal about
2 minutes

each side, or until just
tender.
Remove from dish.
Heat remaining oil in
same dish, cook
eggplant, remove from
dish. Place veal in
dish, top with
eggplant.
Spoon tomato mixture
over eggplant,
sprinkle with cheese.
Bake, uncovered, in
moderate oven about
15 minutes or until
heated through.

Per serve fat 9g; fibre 4g;
kJ 1122

18 pork with prawns
and cucumbers

200g pork fillet

2 large (800g) green cucumbers

400g small cooked shelled prawns

minted dressing

1 1/2 tablespoons lime juice

1 tablespoon fish sauce

1 tablespoon water

1 clove garlic, crushed

1 tablespoon finely shredded mint leaves

1/2 teaspoon sugar

1/2 teaspoon grated lime rind

1/4 teaspoon sambal oelek

Wrap pork tightly in plastic wrap, freeze until partly frozen. Cut pork into 5mm slices. Add pork in batches to pan of boiling water, simmer until just tender; drain on absorbent paper.

Peel cucumbers; slice in half lengthways. Remove and discard seeds, cut cucumbers into thin slices. Just before serving, combine pork, cucumber, prawns and Minted Dressing in large bowl.

Minted Dressing Combine all ingredients in jar.

Per serve fat 5g; fibre 1g; kJ 870

lentil patties with
basil raita

Rinse lentils under cold water, place in medium pan with the water, bring to boil, simmer, covered, about 15 minutes or until all water is absorbed.

Blend or process lentils, soup mix and basil in batches until smooth. Refrigerate 30 minutes. Shape mixture into 8 patties, toss in flour; shake away excess flour.

Heat butter and oil in large pan, cook patties for about 6 minutes each side or until lightly browned. Serve with Basil Raita.

Basil Raita Combine yogurt and basil in small bowl.

1 cup (200g) red lentils

2 cups (500ml) water

70g packet Dutch curry and rice soup mix

1 tablespoon chopped fresh basil leaves

plain flour

30g butter

1 teaspoon olive oil

basil raita

$1/2$ cup low-fat plain yogurt

1 teaspoon chopped fresh basil leaves

Per serve fat 10g; fibre 7g; kJ 1272

rabbit and tarragon
casserole

2 rabbits

1 tablespoon olive oil

12 baby (300g) onions

2 cloves garlic, crushed

1/4 cup (60ml) tomato paste

1 cup (250ml) chicken stock

1 cup (250ml) dry red wine

2 bay leaves

1 teaspoon fresh thyme leaves

2 teaspoons chopped fresh
tarragon leaves

Remove rabbit meat from bones,
cut meat into 2cm pieces. Heat oil
in an 8-cup (2-litre) capacity
flameproof dish, add rabbit, cook,
stirring, until browned all over;
remove dish from heat.

Add remaining ingredients to dish.
Bring to boil, simmer, covered,
about 2 hours or until rabbit is
tender. Discard bay leaves and
serve immediately.

Per serve fat 14g; fibre 2g; kJ 1838

22 layered eggplant
and capsicum salad

3 medium (600g) red capsicums

1kg (about 16) finger eggplants

1 tablespoon olive oil

$^1/_3$ cup (50g) chopped pistachios, toasted

yogurt dressing

1 cup (250ml) low-fat plain yogurt

1 clove garlic, crushed

$^1/_4$ cup chopped fresh coriander leaves

$1^1/_2$ tablespoons chopped fresh oregano leaves

1 teaspoon ground cumin

2 teaspoons honey

Quarter capsicums, remove seeds and membranes. Grill capsicums, skin side up, until skin blisters and blackens. Peel away skin, cut capsicums into thick slices.

Cut eggplants in half lengthways. Heat a little of the oil in large pan, cook eggplant in batches about 5 minutes or until browned all over and very soft; drain on absorbent paper. Add remaining oil to pan and cook remaining eggplant.

Spread quarter of the Yogurt Dressing onto serving plate; top with one-third of the eggplant, then one-third of the capsicum. Repeat layering twice more. Top with remaining Yogurt Dressing; sprinkle with pistachios.

Yogurt Dressing Combine all ingredients in small bowl.

Per serve fat 13g; fibre 9g; kJ 974

creamy coriander
chicken

750g chicken thigh fillets

1 tablespoon peanut oil

1 small fresh red chilli, seeded, chopped

1 medium (150g) brown onion, chopped

1 tablespoon chopped fresh lemon grass

1/3 cup (80ml) light coconut cream

1/4 cup chopped fresh coriander leaves

Cut chicken into 4cm pieces. Heat oil in medium pan, add chilli and onion, stir over heat 5 minutes. Add chicken and lemon grass, cook, stirring, until chicken is cooked through.**Stir** in coconut cream and coriander, simmer, uncovered, 2 minutes.

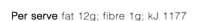

Per serve fat 12g; fibre 1g; kJ 1177

24 lime chicken
on lemon grass skewers

5 x 30cm-long fresh lemon grass stalks

2 teaspoons peanut oil

2 teaspoons grated lime rind

2 tablespoons coarsely chopped fresh coriander leaves

4 (800g) chicken breast fillets

2 tablespoons lime juice

2 small fresh red chillies, seeded, chopped finely

2 teaspoons macadamia oil

1/2 teaspoon raw sugar

1 small clove garlic, crushed

Trim 1 lemon grass stalk and chop finely. Place in large shallow dish with peanut oil, rind and coriander.
Cut each fillet into large chunks and thread onto the 4 lemon grass stalk "skewers". Place skewers in dish, turning to coat chicken in lemon grass marinade. Cover, refrigerate about 3 hours or overnight.
Cover the ends of the lemon grass with foil to prevent them from burning. Cook skewers on heated oiled griddle pan or barbecue, until chicken is browned all over and cooked through. Meanwhile, combine remaining ingredients in jar, shake well. Serve with chicken skewers.

Per serve fat 10g; fibre 1g; kJ 1151

26 pasta with

tomato-bean sauce

375g fresh pasta

tomato-bean sauce

1 tablespoon olive oil

2 cloves garlic, crushed

2 medium (300g) brown onions, chopped

2 bay leaves

2 medium (240g) carrots, chopped

2 celery sticks, chopped

425g can tomatoes

2 tablespoons tomato paste

$1/2$ teaspoon ground cinnamon

445g can butter beans, rinsed, drained

1 cup (250ml) chicken stock

1 tablespoon chopped fresh chives

Gradually add pasta to a large pan of boiling water, boil, uncovered, until pasta is just tender; drain. **Serve** with Tomato-Bean Sauce.
Tomato-Bean Sauce Heat oil in medium pan, add garlic, onion and bay leaves, cook, stirring, until onion is soft. Stir in carrot, celery, undrained crushed tomatoes, paste, cinnamon, beans and stock. Bring to boil, simmer, uncovered, about 10 minutes, or until sauce thickens slightly. Remove from heat; discard bay leaves. Stir in chives.

Per serve fat 6g; fibre 9g; kJ 1029

lamb fillet salad

with spiced chickpeas

2 x 310g cans chickpeas, rinsed, drained

1 teaspoon ground cumin

1 teaspoon ground coriander

1 tablespoon curry powder

1/4 teaspoon chilli powder

2 teaspoons olive oil

500g lamb fillets

salad

1 cup firmly packed flat-leaf parsley, chopped

1/3 cup chopped fresh mint leaves

1 clove garlic, crushed

2 medium (380g) tomatoes, peeled, seeded, chopped

1 (130g) Lebanese cucumber, chopped

tomato cumin dressing

2 teaspoons cumin seeds

410g can tomato puree

2 teaspoons olive oil

1 tablespoon white vinegar

1 tablespoon balsamic vinegar

1 teaspoon seasoned pepper

Toss chickpeas in combined spices and half the oil, spread in single layer on oven tray. Bake, uncovered, in moderately hot oven about 45 minutes or until peas are lightly browned and crisp.
Heat remaining oil in large pan, cook lamb in batches until tender; drain, cover, cool. Slice lamb thinly.
Top Salad with peas and lamb; drizzle with Tomato Cumin Dressing.
Salad Combine all ingredients in small bowl.
Tomato Cumin Dressing Add cumin seeds to dry pan, stir over heat until fragrant. Combine cumin seeds, tomato puree, oil, both vinegars and pepper in jar. Shake well.

Per serve fat 15g; fibre 10g; kJ 1352

capsicums

2 large (600g) potatoes, peeled, grated

3 green onions, chopped finely

1 egg yolk

1/4 cup (30g) soy flour

1 teaspoon ground coriander

2 teaspoons olive oil

roasted capsicums

1 medium (200g) yellow capsicum

1 medium (200g) red capsicum

1/3 cup (55g) burghul

1 1/2 cups finely chopped fresh parsley

2 teaspoons olive oil

1/4 cup (60ml) lemon juice

dressing

1 cup (250ml) low-fat plain yogurt

2 teaspoons ground cumin

3/4 teaspoon ground turmeric

Place potatoes between several sheets of absorbent paper, press paper to remove as much moisture as possible. Combine potatoes, green onion, egg yolk, flour and coriander in large bowl.
Heat oil in large pan, add 1/3 cup potato mixture in batches; flatten to 10cm rounds. Cook cakes slowly until browned underneath, turn, brown other side; drain on absorbent paper; keep warm. Serve topped with Roasted Capsicums; drizzle with Dressing.
Roasted Capsicums Quarter capsicums, remove seeds and membranes. Grill capsicum, skin side up, until skin blisters and blackens; peel away skin, chop capsicums finely. Place burghul in small heatproof bowl, cover with boiling water, stand 20 minutes, drain. Place burghul between several sheets of absorbent paper, press paper to remove as much moisture as possible. Transfer burghul to bowl, add capsicum and remaining ingredients; mix well.
Dressing Combine all ingredients in small bowl.

Per serve fat 7g; fibre 8g; kJ 1134

30 beef with capsicum
on polenta cakes

500g piece beef rump steak,
sliced thinly

2 tablespoons lemon juice

1 teaspoon grated fresh ginger

1 medium (150g) brown
onion, grated

1 tablespoon tomato paste

1 tablespoon soy sauce

1 tablespoon olive oil

1 medium (200g) red capsicum,
sliced thinly

1 medium (150g) brown onion,
sliced, extra

2 teaspoons cornflour

1/2 cup (125ml) chicken stock

4 green onions, chopped

polenta cakes

21/2 cups (625ml) skim milk

11/4 cups (210g) polenta

1/4 cup (210g) grated fresh
parmesan cheese

1/4 cup (20g) chopped fresh parsley

Combine beef, juice, ginger, onion, paste and soy sauce in a large bowl. Cover, refrigerate several hours or overnight.

Heat oil in a wok or large pan, stir-fry capsicum and extra onion, until onion is soft. Remove beef from marinade; reserve marinade. Add beef to wok, stir-fry until well browned all over.

Stir blended cornflour and stock and reserved marinade into wok. Stir over heat until mixture boils and thickens. Remove from heat, stir in green onion. Serve beef and sauce over Polenta Cakes.

Polenta Cakes Oil a 25 x 30cm Swiss roll pan. Pour milk into medium pan; bring to boil. Gradually stir in polenta, reduce heat, simmer, covered, 5 minutes, stirring occasionally. Remove pan from heat, stir in cheese and parsley. Spread mixture evenly into prepared pan.

Bake in moderate oven about 10 minutes, or until polenta is firm. Cut 8 x 8cm rounds from polenta.

Per serve fat 14g; fibre 4g; kJ 2113

a potpourri of
herbs

There are many ways of using herbs: potpourri and herb teas are traditional ways to soothe jagged nerves. And a bunch of herbs mixed with cottage flowers will brighten up any kitchen or bathroom windowsill. Here are a few more ways to use herbs around the house.

Drying herbs

Pick herbs when they're at their peak just before they flower. Early in the morning is the best time to pick, when the dew has dried but before the sun has been on the leaves for too long. Remove large leaves from their stalks; small leaves can be left on and rubbed off after drying. Spread the clean leaves or leaf-bearing stalks, in a single layer, on a piece of gauze or insect screen stretched across a frame and supported so air can circulate freely underneath (between stacked bricks is ideal). The frame should be positioned in a dark, warm, dry place. Dry herbs when the weather is fine, not humid and they should be dried within a week. Store in airtight jars in a cool dry place.

Drying in the microwave

Spread washed and dried fresh leaves on three sheets of absorbent paper and cover with another sheet. Microwave on HIGH (100%) for 2 minutes; remove any herbs that are crisp. Microwave remainder a further 30 seconds or until all herbs are dry. Be careful not to burn them.

Bouquet garni

The traditional bouquet garni is made from bay leaves, parsley and thyme tied together with cotton or kitchen string (one end of which is wound around the handle of the pan for easy retrieving), or they can be tied up together in a little muslin bag. There are variations: the basic bouquet can be placed in the groove of a piece of celery; a piece of orange peel, a clove of garlic, a few celery leaves and a twig or two of fennel can be added to the mix. The bouquet garni adds a delicious flavour to slow-cooking soups and stews. Homemade bouquets using fresh or dry herbs from your garden, muslin squares and string, make a lovely gift.

Fines herbes

Another traditional herb mixture mostly used in omelettes or mixed with melted butter and a squeeze of lemon to be poured over roast chicken or grilled fish. Fines herbes is a delicate blend of finely chopped parsley, chervil, chives and tarragon.

Herb skewers

Use long stems of rosemary as skewers for lamb kebabs, and lemon grass stalks as skewers for chicken or fish pieces. They might frizzle during cooking but this is just a reaction to the herbs' liquid content.

A herb brush

Make a herb brush with a few stalks of flat-leaf parsley, rosemary, tarragon or sage all tied together with kitchen string. Dip this "brush" in oil or marinade and brush over meat before barbecuing or grilling, or use to impart a herby flavour to roasting vegetables.

Herb juice

If you have a juice extractor, process herbs along with the fruit and vegetables. A few mint leaves are delicious added to fresh pineapple juice, and parsley is a great addition to carrot and celery juice. They have the added advantage of freshening the breath: parsley, in particular, is a traditional way of getting rid of garlic on the breath.

■ Use sprigs of sage and stalks of rosemary in your **flower arrangements**. Not only do they look good, they scent the room beautifully.

■ Grow a **pot of basil** in your kitchen to discourage flies.

34 thai beef salad

500g beef rump steak, trimmed
2 (260g) Lebanese cucumbers
5 large (450g) egg tomatoes
160g bean sprouts, trimmed
1 tablespoon small fresh mint leaves

thai dressing
1/4 cup (60ml) sweet chilli sauce
1 tablespoon fish sauce
1 tablespoon lime juice
1 clove garlic, crushed
2 tablespoons chopped fresh coriander leaves
1 tablespoon chopped fresh mint leaves

Brush beef with 1/4 cup (60ml) of the Thai
Dressing. Cover, refrigerate several hours
or overnight.
Cook beef in heated oiled pan until browned
both sides and cooked as desired. Remove
from heat, cover; stand 10 minutes before
slicing thinly. Meanwhile, halve cucumbers
lengthways, scoop out and discard seeds; slice
thinly. Cut tomatoes in quarters lengthways,
remove and discard seeds; slice thinly.
Just before serving, toss beef in medium bowl
with cucumber, tomato, sprouts and remaining
Thai dressing; sprinkle with small mint leaves.
Thai Dressing Combine all ingredients in jar.

Per serve fat 9g; fibre 5g; kJ 1005

36 orange rosemary lamb
cutlets

8 lamb cutlets, trimmed

1 tablespoon olive oil

2 tablespoons honey

1 tablespoon grated orange rind

$^1/_4$ cup (60ml) orange juice

2 tablespoons chopped fresh rosemary

1 clove garlic, crushed

Place cutlets, in single layer, in shallow glass dish. Pour combined remaining ingredients over cutlets; cover, refrigerate 3 hours or overnight. **Drain** cutlets from marinade; reserve marinade. Grill cutlets until browned and cooked through. Pour reserved marinade into small pan. Bring to boil, simmer, 1 minute; pour over cutlets.

Per serve fat 14g; fibre 1g; kJ 1082

veal in herb and
lemon sauce

cooking-oil spray

4 x 125g veal steaks

1/2 cup (125ml) lemon juice

1 tablespoon honey

2 tablespoons brown sugar

1 teaspoon grated fresh ginger

2 cups (500ml) chicken stock

3 teaspoons cornflour

1 tablespoon water

1 tablespoon chopped fresh parsley

1 teaspoon chopped fresh chives

1 teaspoon fresh thyme leaves

Coat a large frying pan with cooking-oil spray, add veal, cook until tender, remove from pan. Add juice, honey, sugar, ginger and stock, bring to the boil, reduce heat, simmer, uncovered, 10 minutes. Stir in blended cornflour and water, stir over heat until mixture boils and thickens. **Add** herbs to sauce, return veal to pan, cook until heated through.

Per serve fat 3g; fibre 0.1g; kJ 890

38 tuna croquettes
with tomato dill sauce

2 medium (400g) potatoes, chopped

425g can tuna in brine, drained

1 medium (150g) brown onion, chopped

4 green onions, chopped

1 egg, beaten lightly

1 medium (120g) carrot, grated

1 tablespoon chopped fresh parsley

plain flour

1 egg white, beaten

1 cup (70g) stale breadcrumbs

1 tablespoon olive oil

tomato dill sauce

2 teaspoons olive oil

1 medium (150g) brown onion, chopped

410g can tomato puree

1 tablespoon chopped fresh dill

2 tablespoons tomato paste

1/2 cup (125ml) dry red wine

Boil, steam or microwave potatoes until tender; drain. Place tuna and potatoes in a large bowl; mash well. Add both onions, egg, carrot and parsley, mix well; refrigerate 30 minutes.

Shape mixture into 12 croquettes, toss in flour, dip into egg white, coat with breadcrumbs; refrigerate 10 minutes.

Heat oil in large pan. Cook croquettes until golden all over and heated through. Serve with Tomato Dill sauce.

Tomato Dill Sauce Heat oil in a medium pan, add onion, cook, stirring, until soft. Add tomato puree with remaining ingredients, bring to the boil, simmer, uncovered, for 5 minutes, or until slightly thickened.

Per serve fat 12g; fibre 6g; kJ 1670

herbed fish
risotto

1 tablespoon olive oil

1 cup (200g) long grain rice

1 1/2 cups (375ml) water

1 tablespoon soy sauce

1 sprig rosemary

410g can tomatoes

400g white fish fillets, chopped

1 celery stick, sliced

1 medium (120g) zucchini, chopped

1 tablespoon chopped fresh chives

2 tablespoons chopped fresh parsley

Heat oil in medium pan, stir in rice, cook, stirring, over high heat, for 5 minutes. Stir in water, sauce, rosemary and undrained crushed tomatoes, bring to boil, simmer, covered, about 15 minutes or until almost all the liquid is absorbed. Remove from heat; discard rosemary.

Stir in fish, celery and zucchini. Cook, covered, for about 5 minutes or until all liquid is absorbed and fish is cooked through. Stir in chives and parsley just before serving.

Per serve fat 8g; fibre 3g; kJ 1493

prawn and scallop
kebabs

16 uncooked king prawns

16 slices prosciutto

32 large basil leaves

16 scallops

1 tablespoon olive oil

lemon juice

Shell and devein prawns, leaving tails intact. Cut prosciutto in half lengthways. Wrap a basil leaf around each prawn and each scallop, then wrap in prosciutto. Thread scallops and prawns onto 8 bamboo skewers.

Heat oil in a large pan, cook kebabs about 3 minutes each side, or until tender. Sprinkle with juice.

Per serve
fat 11g;
fibre 1g;
kJ 1169

trout and garden

vegetable salad

375g smoked trout

¹/₄ cup (60ml) lemon juice

1 medium (200g) green
capsicum, sliced

4 small (360g) zucchini,
sliced

1 (400g) long green
cucumber, sliced

250g cherry tomatoes

6 small (90g)
radishes, halved

dressing

2 tablespoons lemon
juice

2 teaspoons vegetable
oil

1 clove garlic, crushed

1 tablespoon cream

1 tablespoon chopped fresh basil
leaves

Remove skin and bones from trout. Flake trout into
large pieces.
Combine trout, juice, capsicum, zucchini, cucumber, tomatoes and radish
in large bowl. Add Dressing just before serving.
Dressing Combine all ingredients in jar.

Per serve fat 10g; fibre 4g; kJ 903

cantonese
lamb patties

4 Chinese dried mushrooms

2 teaspoons peanut oil

1 small (80g) brown onion, chopped finely

1 tablespoon finely chopped lemon grass

2 cloves garlic, crushed

1 tablespoon finely grated fresh ginger

750g lean minced lamb

3 green onions, chopped

1 tablespoon soy sauce

1 tablespoon hoisin sauce

1/4 teaspoon sesame oil

1 egg, beaten

1/2 cup (35g) stale breadcrumbs

120g bean sprouts

1/4 cup (60ml) sweet chilli sauce

1 tablespoon water

1 tablespoon lime juice

1 tablespoon finely chopped fresh coriander leaves

Place mushrooms in small heatproof bowl, cover with boiling water, stand 20 minutes; drain. Remove and discard stems; chop caps finely. Heat peanut oil in large pan; cook brown onion, lemon grass, garlic and ginger, stirring, until onion is soft.

Combine mushroom and onion mixture in large bowl with lamb, green onion, sauces, sesame oil, egg and breadcrumbs.

Shape mixture into 8 patties; cook, in batches, in large heated oiled pan until browned both sides and cooked through. Serve with sprouts and drizzled with combined remaining ingredients.

Per serve fat 14g; fibre 2g; kJ 1151

44 mussels in
tomato caper sauce

2 kg mussels

1 tablespoon olive oil

1 clove garlic, crushed

1 medium (150g) brown onion, chopped

2 small fresh red chillies, chopped finely

1/4 cup (60ml) tomato paste

1/4 cup (60ml) dry white wine

425g can tomatoes

2 teaspoons sugar

1 tablespoon drained capers, chopped

2 tablespoons chopped fresh basil leaves

Scrub mussels, remove beards. Heat oil in large pan, add garlic, onion and chilli, cook, stirring, until onion is soft. Stir in paste, wine, undrained crushed tomatoes, sugar and capers. **Bring** to boil, simmer, uncovered, until sauce thickens slightly. Stir in basil. Add mussels, bring to boil; simmer, covered, until shells open. Discard any unopened mussels.

Per serve fat 8g; fibre 3g; kJ 820

port and garlic
beef

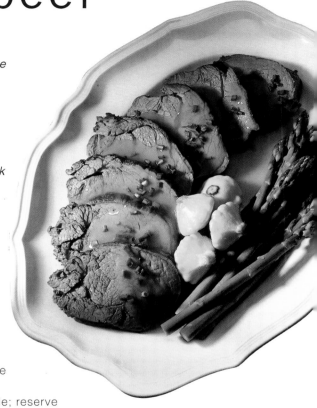

1 tablespoon port

2 teaspoons dark soy sauce

$1/2$ teaspoon vegetable oil

2 cloves garlic, crushed

500g piece beef eye fillet

chive sauce

1 cup (250ml) chicken stock

1 teaspoon tomato paste

1 tablespoon lemon juice

2 teaspoons cornflour

1 tablespoon water

1 tablespoon chopped
fresh chives

Combine port, sauce, oil and garlic in large bowl,. Add beef; turn to coat with marinade. Cover, refrigerate overnight.

Remove beef from marinade; reserve marinade. Tie beef with string to keep in shape. Place beef in baking dish.

Bake in moderately hot oven for about 40 minutes or until beef is cooked as desired. Cover beef, stand 5 minutes before carving, serve with the Chive Sauce.

Chive Sauce Combine stock, paste, juice and reserved marinade in small pan. Stir in blended cornflour and water. Stir over heat until sauce boils and thickens slightly. Add chives just before serving.

Per serve fat 5g; fibre 1g; kJ 732

46 tortellini and
tomato soup

300g beef tortellini

2 teaspoons olive oil

2 medium (300g) brown onions, chopped finely

1 bacon rasher, chopped

2 cloves garlic, crushed

2 x 400g cans tomatoes

1/4 cup (60ml) dry red wine

1 1/2 cups (375ml) chicken stock

2 tablespoons tomato paste

1 teaspoon sugar

1 tablespoon chopped fresh basil leaves

1 teaspoon fresh thyme leaves

2 tablespoons shaved parmesan cheese

olive and basil muffins

cooking-oil spray

3/4 cup (105g) self-raising flour

1/2 teaspoon bicarbonate of soda

1 1/4 cups (210g) polenta

1/3 cup (55g) chopped pitted black olives

1/4 cup (20g) finely grated parmesan cheese

1/3 cup chopped fresh basil leaves

1 tablespoon chopped fresh chives

1 1/2 cups (375ml) buttermilk

2 egg whites

Add tortellini to large pan of boiling water, boil, uncovered, until just tender; drain.
Heat oil in large pan, add onion, bacon and garlic, cook, stirring, about 5 minutes or until onion is soft. Add undrained crushed tomatoes, wine, stock, paste and sugar. Bring to boil, simmer, covered, 10 minutes. Stir in tortellini and herbs.

Top with cheese, serve with Olive and Basil Muffins.
Olive and Basil Muffins Coat 12 holes of muffin pan (1/3 cup/80ml capacity) with cooking-oil spray. Sift flour and soda into large bowl, stir in polenta, olives, cheese, herbs, buttermilk and egg whites, mix until just combined; do not over-mix. Spoon mixture into prepared pan, sprinkle with a little extra polenta. Bake in moderately hot oven about 20 minutes.

Per serve fat 14g; fibre 9g; kJ 2404

48 chicken in garlic
sauce

750g chicken thigh fillets

1 tablespoon olive oil

4 cloves garlic, crushed

4 green onions, chopped

1 tablespoon plain flour

1 cup (250ml) chicken stock

1/4 cup (60ml) dry red wine

1/4 cup chopped fresh parsley

1 teaspoon chopped fresh thyme leaves

Cut chicken into thin strips. Heat oil in pan, add chicken, cook, stirring, until lightly browned and tender. Add garlic and onion, cook, stirring, until onion is soft. Add flour, cook, stirring, until combined. Remove from heat, gradually stir in stock and wine.

Stir over heat until mixture boils, simmer, uncovered, about 2 minutes or until thickened slightly; stir in herbs.

Per serve fat 13g; fibre 1g; kJ 1302

rosemary pork

with mandarin sauce

1 tablespoon olive oil

600g pork fillet

1 cup (250ml) chicken stock

2 tablespoons Grand Marnier

3 teaspoons cornflour

2 tablespoons water

1 cup (250ml) mandarin juice

1 tablespoon chopped fresh rosemary

Heat oil in large pan, cook pork until browned all over. Place pork on rack in baking dish. Heat stock and liqueur in small pan. Bring to boil, pour into baking dish.

Bake, covered, in moderate oven, about 20 minutes or until pork is tender. Remove pork from rack; cover to keep warm.

Stir blended cornflour and water with juice into dish, stir over heat until mixture boils and thickens, stir in rosemary. Serve pork with sauce.

Per serve fat 8g; fibre 1g; kJ 1053

50 olive, tomato
and chilli salad

4 medium (300g) egg
tomatoes

1 small (100g) red
onion

2 1/2 cups (400g) pitted
black olives

3 cups (150g) firmly
packed watercress
sprigs

120g rocket

1/4 cup (40g) drained
bottled hot red chillies

1 tablespoon chopped
fresh coriander leaves

dressing

1 tablespoon olive oil

2 teaspoons lemon
juice

1/2 teaspoon chopped
fresh rosemary

1 teaspoon cumin
seeds

2 cloves garlic,
crushed

Cut tomatoes into
wedges. Slice onion,
separate into rings.
Combine tomatoes,
onion, olives,
watercress, rocket
and chillies in large
bowl. Drizzle with
Dressing; top with
coriander.
Dressing Combine all
ingredients in jar.

Per serve fat 9g; fibre 9g;
kJ 590

pepper and rosemary
chicken kebabs

750g chicken thigh fillets

1/2 cup (125ml) lemon juice

1/2 teaspoon cracked black pepper

1 clove garlic, crushed

2 tablespoons chopped fresh rosemary

1 tablespoon chopped fresh basil leaves

1 tablespoon olive oil

Cut chicken into 3cm pieces. Combine chicken, juice, pepper, garlic, rosemary and basil in medium bowl. Cover, refrigerate several hours or overnight.

Drain chicken; reserve marinade. Thread chicken onto 8 skewers. Heat oil in large pan, add kebabs, cook, turning occasionally, until lightly browned and cooked through. Add reserved marinade, bring to boil, turn kebabs to coat in marinade.

Per serve fat 13g; fibre 1g; kJ 1177

52 rosemary
lamb casserole

1 tablespoon olive oil

750g lean diced lamb

1 medium (150g) brown onion, sliced

2 cloves garlic, crushed

1/2 cup (125ml) dry red wine

1 1/2 cups (375ml) beef stock

1/4 cup (60ml) redcurrant jelly

1 tablespoon chopped fresh rosemary

1/2 cup pitted prunes, halved

3 teaspoons cornflour

1 tablespoon water

Heat oil in 6-cup (1.5 litre) capacity flameproof dish, cook lamb in batches, stirring, until well browned all over; remove from pan. Add onion and garlic to same pan, cook, stirring, about 5 minutes or until onion is soft. Add wine, stock, jelly, rosemary, prunes and lamb, simmer, uncovered, 5 minutes.

Bake, covered, in moderate oven 1 hour. Stir in blended cornflour and water, bake, uncovered, further 30 minutes or until lamb is tender and sauce is thickened.

Per serve fat 12g; fibre 3g; kJ 1644

prawn, bean and
mushroom salad

300g button mushrooms, sliced

300g green beans, chopped

1kg cooked king prawns

2 tablespoons chopped fresh
chives

dressing

1/4 cup (60ml) brown vinegar

1 tablespoon oil

1/4 cup (60ml) no-oil French
dressing

1 teaspoon cracked black
peppercorns

1 clove garlic, crushed

Combine mushrooms and Dressing
in a medium bowl, toss well. Cover
bowl, stand 30 minutes. Boil,
steam or microwave beans until
just tender, drain, rinse under cold
water; drain.
Shell and devein prawns, leaving
tails intact. Add prawns, beans
and chives to mushroom mixture.
Dressing Combine all ingredients
in jar.

Per serve fat 7g; fibre 4g; kJ 911

54 fish steaks with dill and caper sauce

4 (1kg) white fish steaks

plain flour

1 tablespoon olive oil

dill and caper sauce

2 teaspoons olive oil

1 small (80g) brown onion, chopped

1/2 teaspoon drained capers, chopped

2 cups (500ml) tomato juice

1 teaspoon sugar

2 teaspoons cornflour

1 tablespoon water

1 tablespoon chopped fresh dill

Toss fish steaks in flour, shake away excess flour. Heat oil in large pan, add fish, cook about 3 minutes each side, or until cooked through. Serve with Dill and Caper sauce.

Dill and Caper Sauce Heat oil in small pan, add onion, cook, stirring, 5 minutes or until onion is soft. Add capers, juice and sugar, simmer, uncovered, 10 minutes. Stir in blended cornflour and water, stir over heat until sauce boils and thickens slightly. Stir in dill.

Per serve fat 15g; fibre 1g; kJ 1672

carrot kofta
with lentil sauce

1 kg medium carrots, grated finely

1 cup (150g) plain flour

2 tablespoons chopped fresh coriander leaves

1 teaspoon ground coriander

1/4 teaspoon cayenne pepper

lentil sauce

40g butter

1 medium (150g) brown onion, chopped finely

1 clove garlic, crushed

2 teaspoons garam masala

1 teaspoon turmeric

1/4 teaspoon cayenne pepper

1 cup (200g) red lentils

410g can tomato puree

1.25 litres (5 cups) water

Combine carrot, flour, fresh and ground coriander and pepper in a large bowl.
Shape mixture into 20 balls, place on tray, cover, refrigerate for at least 30 minutes.
Place carrot balls into simmering Lentil Sauce, cover, simmer 15 minutes.
Lentil Sauce Heat butter in large pan, add onion, garlic, garam masala, turmeric and pepper, cook, stirring, until onion is soft. Add lentils, cook, stirring, 2 minutes. Add remaining ingredients, bring to boil, simmer, uncovered 30 minutes or until lentils are soft.

Per serve fat 10g; fibre 19g; kJ 1823

You will need a medium-size oven bag for this recipe.

1 rabbit

40g butter

$^1/_4$ cup (40g) pine nuts

1 medium (150g) brown onion, chopped finely

1 celery stick, chopped

1 cup (70g) stale white breadcrumbs

1 teaspoon grated lemon rind

2 tablespoons finely chopped fresh parsley

1 teaspoon chopped fresh thyme leaves

1 teaspoon chopped fresh sage leaves

1 tablespoon dried currants

4 bacon rashers

1 tablespoon plain flour

$^1/_2$ cup (125ml) chicken stock

$^1/_4$ cup (60ml) dry sherry

1 tablespoon soy sauce

1 tablespoon hoisin sauce

Wash rabbit well; pat dry with absorbent paper. Melt butter in small pan, add pine nuts and onion, cook until onion is soft. Combine onion mixture, celery, breadcrumbs, rind, parsley, thyme, sage and currants in medium bowl. Mix well.

Fill cavity of rabbit with this seasoning, secure opening with skewers. Wrap bacon around rabbit, secure with skewers. Place flour in oven bag, shake well; place rabbit in bag; put bag in baking dish. Pour combined stock, sherry and sauces over rabbit in bag. Secure bag with tie provided, slit bag several times near tie.

Bake in moderate oven about 1$^1/_2$ hours or until rabbit is tender, turning occasionally. Remove rabbit from bag, remove skewers. Cut rabbit into quarters and serve with sauce from oven bag.

Per serve fat 14g; fibre 3g; kJ 1478

3 medium (600g) red capsicums

2 large (360g) parsnips

1 tablespoon olive oil

3 cloves garlic, crushed

6 cardamom pods, bruised

3 teaspoons ground cumin

1 teaspoon brown mustard seeds

1 teaspoon cumin seeds

1 teaspoon ground coriander

1 bunch (400g) baby carrots

4 small (360g) zucchini, halved

2 cups (320g) burghul

2¹/₂ cups (625ml) boiling chicken stock

basil dressing

1 cup (250ml) low-fat plain yogurt

1 cup firmly packed fresh basil leaves

Cut capsicums into 3cm strips. Cut parsnips into wedges. **Heat** oil in large flameproof dish, add garlic and spices; stir over heat until fragrant. Add all vegetables, stir until coated with spice mixture. Bake uncovered, in hot oven about 45 minutes, turning vegetables occasionally, until they are tender and lightly browned.

Place burghul in medium heatproof bowl, add stock, stand 30 minutes or until stock is absorbed. Serve roasted vegetables with burghul and Basil Dressing.

Basil Dressing Blend or process yogurt and basil until smooth.

Per serve fat 8g; fibre 23g; kJ 1876

glossary

bean sprouts also known as bean shoots; tender new growths of assorted beans and seeds germinated for consumption as sprouts. The most readily available are mung bean, soy bean, alfalfa and snow pea sprouts.

bok choy also called pak choi or Chinese white cabbage; has a fresh, mild mustard taste and is good braised or in stir-fries. Baby bok choy is also available.

breadcrumbs, stale 1- or 2-day-old bread made into crumbs by grating, blending or processing.

burghul wheat that is steamed until partly cooked, cracked then dried.

butter beans also called cannellini beans, small white beans, available dried or canned.

buttermilk low-fat milk cultured with bacteria to give it a slightly sour, tangy taste.

capers pickled buds of a Mediterranean shrub. The smaller the better.

capsicum also known as bell pepper. Seeds and membranes should be discarded before use.

chickpeas also called garbanzos or channa; an irregularly round, sandy-coloured legume used extensively in Mediterranean cooking.

chilli sauce, sweet a comparatively mild Thai-type commercial sauce made from red chillies, sugar, garlic and vinegar.

coconut cream, light made from coconut and water, available in cans.

cooking-oil spray vegetable oil in an aerosol can, available in supermarkets.

cornflour also known as cornstarch.

cucumber, Lebanese small green cucumber.

dressing, no-oil French bottled dressing available in supermarkets.

Dutch curry and rice soup mix sachet of mild creamy curry soup mix.

eggplants, finger small, finger-length eggplants (aubergine).

fish sauce also called nam pla or nuoc nam; made from pulverised salted fermented fish, most often anchovies. Has a pungent smell and strong taste; use sparingly.

flour, soy made from ground soy beans.

garam masala a blend of spices based on cardamom, cinnamon, cloves, coriander, fennel and cumin, roasted and ground together.

hoisin sauce a thick, sweet and spicy Chinese paste made from salted fermented soy beans, onions and garlic. Use as a marinade or baste.

macadamia oil oil extracted from macadamia nuts. Use sparingly.

milk, evaporated skim unsweetened canned skim milk from which water has been extracted by evaporation. It has 0.3 percent fat content.

mushrooms, Chinese dried soak in warm water, remove stalks, slice caps. Unique in flavour.

mussels should be bought from a fish market where there is reliably fresh fish. They must be tightly closed when bought, indicating they are alive. Before cooking, scrub the shells with a strong brush and remove the "beards". Discard any mussels that do not open after cooking.

mustard, seeded a French-style textured mustard made with crushed mustard seeds.

oil, sesame used throughout Asia, made from roasted, crushed white sesame seeds; used as a flavouring rather than a cooking medium.

onion, green also known as scallion or (incorrectly) as shallot; an immature onion picked before the bulb has formed, having a long, bright-green edible stalk.

pine nuts also called pignoli; small cream-coloured kernels.

pistachios pale green, delicately flavoured nut inside hard shell. To peel, soak shelled nuts in boiling water for 5 minutes; drain, then pat dry with absorbent paper. Rub skins off with cloth.

polenta a flour-like cereal made from ground corn (maize); similar to cornmeal but coarser and darker in colour.

prosciutto salt-cured, air-dried (unsmoked) pressed ham; usually sold in paper-thin slices, ready to eat.

sambal oelek (also ulek or olek) Indonesian in origin; a salty paste made from ground chillies, sugar and spices.

snow peas also called mangetout ("eat all").

tofu made from boiled, crushed soy beans; also known as beancurd. We used firm tofu in this book. Buy tofu as fresh as possible; keep any leftover tofu in the refrigerator under water; change water daily.

vinegar
  balsamic: authentic only from the province of Modena, Italy; made from a regional wine of white Trebbiano grapes specially processed then aged in antique wooden casks to give its exquisite flavour.
  brown: made made from fermented malt and beech shavings.

wasabi paste extremely hot green horseradish, available from Asian food stores.

zucchini also known as courgette.

index

facts and figures 63

These conversions are approximate only, but the difference between an exact and the approximate conversion of various liquid and dry measures is minimal and will not affect your cooking results.

Measuring equipment

The difference between one country's measuring cups and another's is, at most, within a 2 or 3 teaspoon variance. (For the record, 1 Australian metric measuring cup holds approximately 250ml.) The most accurate way of measuring dry ingredients is to weigh them. For liquids, use a clear glass or plastic jug having metric markings.

Note: NZ, Canada, USA and UK all use 15ml tablespoons. Australian tablespoons measure 20ml.
All cup and spoon measurements are level.

How to measure

When using graduated measuring cups, shake dry ingredients loosely into the appropriate cup. Do not tap the cup on a bench or tightly pack the ingredients unless directed to do so. Level the top of measuring cups and measuring spoons with a knife. When measuring liquids, place a clear glass or plastic jug having metric markings on a flat surface to check accuracy at eye level.

Dry Measures

metric	imperial
15g	1/2oz
30g	1oz
60g	2oz
90g	3oz
125g	4oz (1/4lb)
155g	5oz
185g	6oz
220g	7oz
250g	8oz (1/2lb)
280g	9oz
315g	10oz
345g	11oz
375g	12oz (3/4lb)
410g	13oz
440g	14oz
470g	15oz
500g	16oz (1lb)
750g	24oz (1 1/2lb)
1kg	32oz (2lb)

We use large eggs having an average weight of 60g.

Liquid Measures

metric	imperial
30ml	1 fluid oz
60ml	2 fluid oz
100ml	3 fluid oz
125ml	4 fluid oz
150ml	5 fluid oz (1/4 pint/1 gill)
190ml	6 fluid oz
250ml (1cup)	8 fluid oz
300ml	10 fluid oz (1/2 pint)
500ml	16 fluid oz
600ml	20 fluid oz (1 pint)
1000ml (1litre)	1 3/4 pints

Helpful Measures

metric	imperial
3mm	1/8in
6mm	1/4in
1cm	1/2in
2cm	3/4in
2.5cm	1in
6cm	2 1/2in
8cm	3in
20cm	8in
23cm	9in
25cm	10in
30cm	12in (1ft)

Oven Temperatures

These oven temperatures are only a guide.
Always check the manufacturer's manual.

	C°(Celsius)	F°(Fahrenheit)	Gas Mark
Very slow	120	250	1
Slow	150	300	2
Moderately slow	160	325	3
Moderate	180 –190	350 – 375	4
Moderately hot	200 – 210	400 – 425	5
Hot	220 – 230	450 – 475	6
Very hot	240 – 250	500 – 525	7

Food editor Pamela Clark
Associate food editor Karen Hammial
Assistant food editor Kathy McGarry
Assistant recipe editor Elizabeth Hooper

HOME LIBRARY STAFF
Editor-in-chief Mary Coleman
Marketing manager Nicole Pizanis
Editor Susan Tomnay
Concept design Jackie Richards
Designer Sue de Guingand
Group publisher Paul Dykzeul
Chief executive officer John Alexander

Produced by The Australian Women's Weekly
Home Library, Sydney.

Colour separations by
ACP Colour Graphics Pty Ltd, Sydney.
Printing by Diamond Press Limited, Sydney.

Published by ACP Publishing Pty Limited,
54 Park St, Sydney; GPO Box 4088, Sydney,
NSW 1028. Ph: (02) 9282 8618
Fax: (02) 9267 9438.

AWWHomeLib@publishing.acp.com.au

Australia Distributed by Network Distribution
Company, GPO Box 4088, Sydney, NSW 1028.
Ph: (02) 9282 8777 Fax: (02) 9264 3278.

United Kingdom Distributed by Australian
Consolidated Press (UK), Moulton Park
Business Centre, Red House Rd, Moulton Park,
Northampton, NN3 6AQ. Ph: (01604) 497 531
Fax: (01604) 497 533 Acpukltd@aol.com

Canada Distributed by Whitecap Books Ltd,
351 Lynn Ave, North Vancouver, BC, V7J 2C4,
(604) 980 9852.

New Zealand Distributed by Netlink Distribution
Company, 17B Hargreaves St,
Level 5, College Hill, Auckland 1, (9) 302 7616.

South Africa Distributed by PSD Promotions
(Pty) Ltd,PO Box 1175, Isando 1600, SA,
(011) 392 6065.

Healthy Eating: Herbs

Includes index.
ISBN 1 86396 146 1.

1Cookery (Herbs). I Title: Australian Women's
Weekly. (Series: Australian Women's Weekly
healthy eating mini series).
641.568

© ACP Publishing Pty Limited 1999
ACN 053 273 546

Cover Lime chicken on lemon grass skewers,
page 24.
Stylist Michelle Noeranto
Photographer Brett Danton
Back cover Thai beef salad, page 34

In the series
healthy eating
make it tonight
sweet and simple
creative food